P9-CWD-663

LIFE IN STRANGE PLACES

Itty Gritty Critters
life between grains of sand

Harry Breidahl

This edition first published in 2002 in the United States of America by Chelsea House Publishers, a subsidiary of Haights Cross Communications.

Chelsea House Publishers
1974 Sproul Road, Suite 400
Broomall, PA 19008-0914

The Chelsea House world wide web address is www.chelseahouse.com

Library of Congress Cataloging-in-Publication Data Applied for.
ISBN 0-7910-6615-0

First published in 2001 by
Macmillan Education Australia Pty Ltd
627 Chapel Street, South Yarra, Australia, 3141

Copyright © Harry Breidahl 2001

Edited by Angelique Campbell-Muir
Text design by Cristina Neri
Cover design by Cristina Neri
Desktop publishing by Cristina Neri
Illustrations by Rhyll Plant
Printed in China

Acknowledgements
The author and the publishers are grateful to the following for permission to reproduce copyright material:

Cover photographs: Rippled sand background, courtesy PhotoDisc; water bear, courtesy Photolibrary.com/David Scharf/SPL; meiofaunal copepod, courtesy Genefor Walker-Smith.

Auscape/Becca Saunders, p. 26; Auscape/John Cancalosi, p. 8 (left); Auscape/Tina Carvalho — Oxford Scientific Films, p. 9 (bottom left); Coo-ee Picture Library, p. 29 (right); Genefor Walker-Smith, pp. 3, 4 (bottom left), 4–5 (top), 14, 24, 27 (both); Gustaaf M. Hallegraeff/University of Tasmania , p. 11 (bottom right); Harry Breidahl, pp. 11 (top left), 16; National Oceanic and Atmospheric Administration/Department of Commerce/Neil Sullivan, University of Southern California, p. 9 (middle right); PhotoDisc, pp. 9 (top left), 10; Photolibrary.com/David Scharf/SPL, pp. 1, 4 (bottom right), 5 (bottom right), 12, 19, 22; Photolibrary.com/John Walsh/SPL, pp. 5 (top right), 17; Photolibrary.com/Philippe Plailly/SPL, pp. 6–7 (top), 25 (bottom right); Photolibrary.com/Trevor Worden, p. 8 (right); Reinhardt Kristensen, pp. 5 (bottom left), 18, 20; Stephen Doggett/Department of Medical Entomology, Westmead Hospital, pp. 7, 25 (top left); The Picture Source/Janet Gwyther, p. 29 (left).

Contents

SEARCHING THE WORLD WIDE WEB

If you have access to the world wide web, you usually have a gateway to some fascinating information. At this time, though, there is not a lot of information about meiofauna on the web. Nevertheless, if you search very carefully you should be able to find some useful information. In this book, useful search words appear like this— ✷ tardigrade. Useful books and web sites are also listed on page 30.

Introducing meiofauna

Biologists use the name ✒ meiofauna to describe a special group of very small organisms. Meiofauna are officially defined as 'being able to pass through a 1 millimeter mesh sieve but are retained by a 0.042 millimeter mesh sieve'. This means, meiofauna are organisms between 1 millimeter and 0.042 millimeter in size.

Meiofauna can be found in many aquatic (water) environments. This book will concentrate on meiofauna that live in the spaces between grains of marine sediments and freshwater sediments. Just a handful of beach sand can hold thousands of these animals. Some are small members of animal groups that biologists already know; others are new to science.

Meiofauna living in the spaces between sand grains can be washed off and collected in a fine sieve. However, you will need a microscope to see them (see pages 24–25).

HOW DO YOU SAY IT?

meiofauna: mi-**o**-fawn-er

✒ Roundworms are the most common members of the meiofaunal world. Their long, thin bodies are ideally suited to life between sand grains (see pages 12–13).

Small 🖈 copepods are also common inhabitants of the spaces between sand grains. Copepods belong to a group of animals that are also found in other environments (see pages 14–15).

HOW DO YOU SAY IT?

copepod: co-**pee**-pod
rotifer: **row**-tif-er

🖈 Rotifers and 🖈 flatworms are also found in other environments, and were known to biologists before the world of meiofauna was discovered and explored (see pages 16–17).

There are many worm-like members of the meiofaunal community. Because a long, thin body is ideal for life between sand grains, many of these worm-like animals live only as meiofauna (see pages 18–19).

🖈 Water bears never grow to more than 1 millimeter long, and therefore they only live as meiofauna. These delightful little animals can survive in conditions that would kill many other animals (see pages 22–23).

Background
Measuring meiofauna

To get an idea of just how small the inhabitants of the meiofaunal world are, you need to think about scale and measurement. The measurement units used in this book belong to the metric system. In the metric system, the smallest commonly used unit is a millimeter (mm). (If you are used to feet and inches, 100 millimeters equals about 4 inches.) A human eye can see objects as small as one-tenth of a millimeter across—any smaller than that and you would need a magnifying glass or a microscope to see clearly.

Because meiofauna are so small, you also need to be familiar with the units of measurement used for anything smaller than a millimeter. This is where the metric system is easy to follow because each new unit is smaller by a factor of 10, 100 or 1,000. Counting down in lots of 1,000, there are two important metric units of measurement that you need to remember:

- one millimeter (mm) is $^1/_{1000}$ of a meter
- one micrometer (μm) is $^1/_{1000}$ of a millimeter

Meiofauna are really small—smaller than 1 millimeter but bigger than 42 micrometers (0.042 millimeter).

human eye

1 mm
1000 μm

10 mm
1 cm

water bear

Illustrations not drawn to scale.

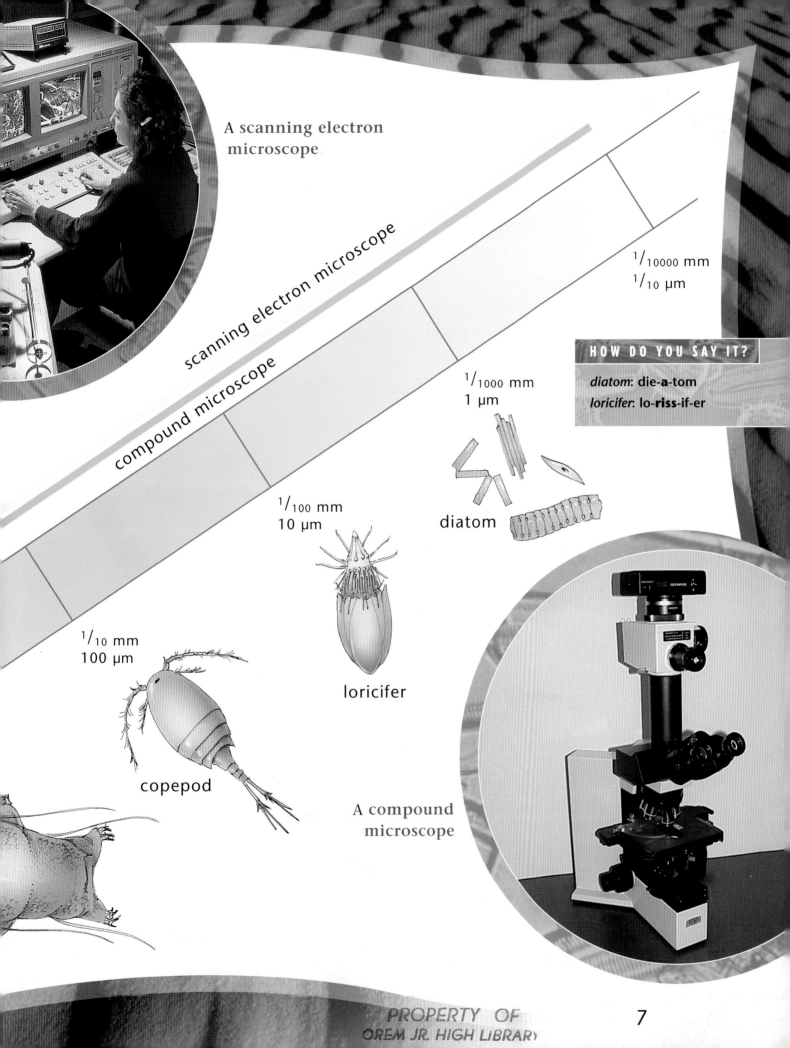

A scanning electron
microscope

scanning electron microscope

compound microscope

$1/10000$ mm
$1/10$ µm

$1/1000$ mm
1 µm

HOW DO YOU SAY IT?

diatom: **die-a-tom**
loricifer: **lo-riss-if-er**

diatom

$1/100$ mm
10 µm

loricifer

$1/10$ mm
100 µm

copepod

A compound
microscope

Sorting life on Earth into kingdoms

Until quite recently biologists divided life on Earth into two broad groups—the plant kingdom and the animal kingdom. The main difference between these two groups is that plants stay in one place and usually make their own food, while animals move about and feed on other organisms.

Since the discovery of microscopic organisms, this simple two-kingdom system is no longer used. One new classification system sorts life on Earth into five kingdoms. Meiofauna belong to the Kingdom Animalia.

Kingdom Animalia

Animals are organisms that eat other organisms. We normally think of animals as being large enough to see, but meiofauna are animals that are too small to see without a microscope. Biologists are only just beginning to study the microscopic world of meiofauna.

Kingdom Plantae

Plants are organisms that use sunlight to make their own food. Trees, grasses, ferns and mosses belong to the plant kingdom (seaweeds are now in the Kingdom Protoctista). Some meiofauna live on mosses and seagrasses.

Kingdom Fungi

Fungi, such as mushrooms and toadstools, were once thought to be plants. Now they are placed in a kingdom of their own. They get their energy by decomposing (breaking down) other organisms. Microscopic marine fungi break down **organic** material in the world of meiofauna.

Kingdom Protoctista

Most members of this kingdom are microscopic. Some are animal-like because they eat other organisms. Others have the plant-like ability to make their own food. Diatoms and dinoflagellates, two members of the Kingdom Protoctista, are important food producers for meiofauna.

Kingdom Monera

The members of the Kingdom Monera are all microscopic organisms called microbes. Another name for them is **bacteria**. In the world of meiofauna, some bacteria break down organic material. Other bacteria can make their own food from sunlight.

HOW DO YOU SAY IT?

dinoflagellate: dine-o-**fla**-jell-ate
protoctista: pro-toe-**tiss**-ta
monera: **mon**-ear-a

9

Living between sand grains

To see what it would be like to live as a member of the meiofaunal world you can look closely at the shoreline of a sandy beach. Although you cannot see it, there is living space between the grains of sand. To see this for yourself, try stacking a number of tennis balls together. You will find there is plenty of space between the balls. The same is true for the sand grains.

Meiofauna live in the spaces between the sand grains. They get food from a number of sources. They can eat microscopic food particles that are carried to the shore by waves and currents. These food particles could be **phytoplankton**, or the remains of other small sea creatures. Meiofauna can also feed on microscopic diatoms and dinoflagellates that live on the sand grains. Meiofauna may also eat each other.

HOW DO YOU SAY IT?

phytoplankton: fite-o-**plank**-ton

Most humans are not thinking about wildlife when they take a trip to the beach. However, at the water's edge, the sand beneath your feet may be full of life. Although they are too small to see, whole communities of meiofauna live between the sand grains.

Look closely at the shoreline of a sandy beach at low tide. You may notice signs of life in the sand. Not all life here is meiofaunal, though. Some signs, such as squiggles and minute holes, are produced by animals that are too large to be called meiofauna.

Diatoms are microscopic members of the Kingdom Protoctista. Many diatoms drift about the ocean as ✦ phytoplankton while others can live on the surface of sand grains. They use sunlight to make their own food, creating minute 'gardens' upon which meiofauna feed.

Meiofauna
Roundworms

If you go back to the tennis ball model of the meiofaunal world, you will see that there is plenty of space between the sand grains on a beach. When you look closely, though, you will see that moving about in these spaces is going to be difficult. You should also be able to see that a long, thin body would be the most suited to moving through these narrow spaces.

So, it should not be a surprise to learn that the most common types of meiofauna are worm-like animals called ✪ roundworms. Roundworms are also known as ✪ nematodes or ✪ threadworms. Roundworms are one of the most common animals on Earth. They are found in many different environments. Many live on plants and animals as **parasites**. Others live in places such as the soil or beach sand.

Roundworms that live between sand grains can be as small as 100 micrometers long. To get a close-up view of something this small you would need an electron microscope.

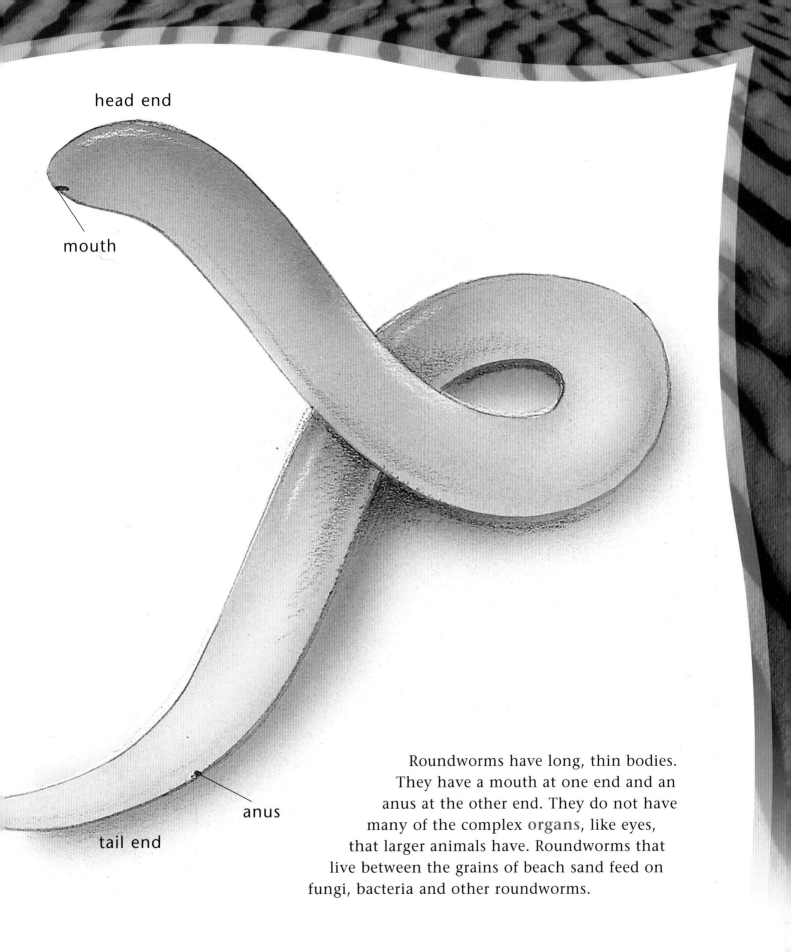

head end

mouth

anus

tail end

Roundworms have long, thin bodies.
They have a mouth at one end and an
anus at the other end. They do not have
many of the complex **organs**, like eyes,
that larger animals have. Roundworms that
live between the grains of beach sand feed on
fungi, bacteria and other roundworms.

copepods

Minute animals called ✪ copepods are another very common member of the meiofaunal world. Copepods live in both freshwater and marine environments. In fact, they are by far the most abundant animals in the sea. Many copepods are free-living, but at least one-third live as parasites on other animals. The best-known copepods drift about in water. They are part of a community known as **plankton**. The copepods that live between sand grains and in other places are less well known.

Copepods have a protective shell and belong to the same animal group as crabs and shrimp. This animal group is called the Crustacea. Like all other **crustaceans**, copepods have a body that is divided into three sections. The head and the middle section (thorax) are joined and the end section (abdomen) is divided into segments. Copepods usually have one eye, two pairs of antennae and a number of jointed legs. Planktonic copepods are usually a teardrop shape and have long antennae. Copepods that live as meiofauna are usually long and thin, with short antennae and legs.

A scanning electron microscope is used to make very detailed pictures of meiofauna, such as the copepod shown here. These microscopes give clear pictures of small organisms.

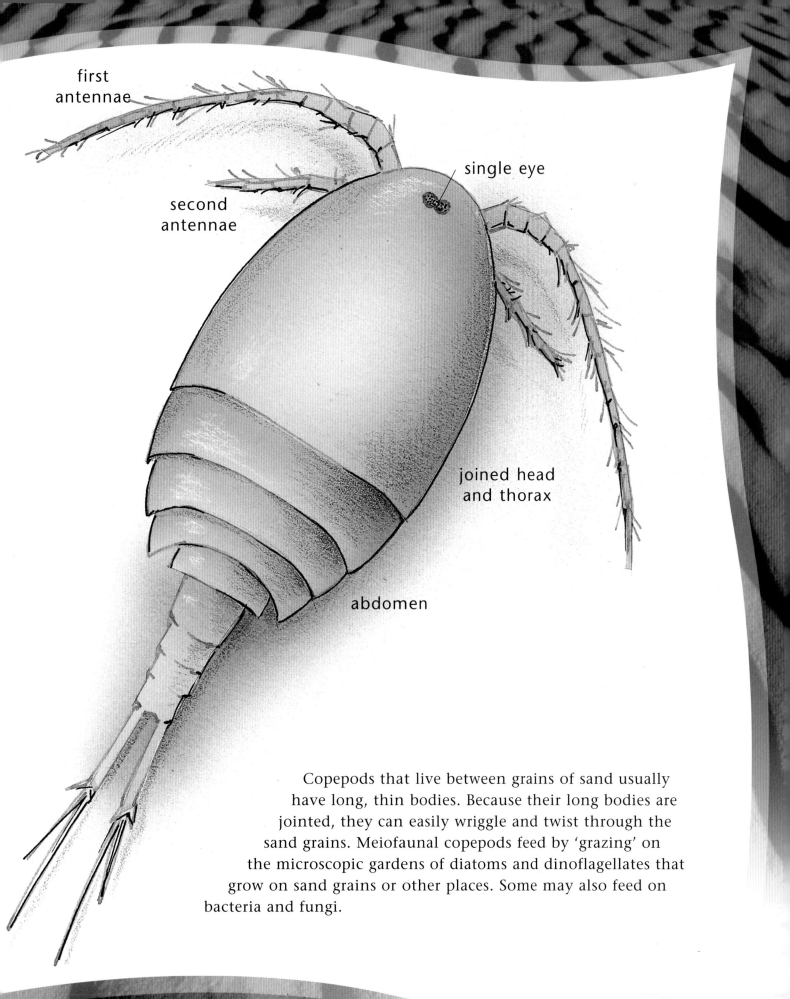

first
antennae

second
antennae

single eye

joined head
and thorax

abdomen

Copepods that live between grains of sand usually
have long, thin bodies. Because their long bodies are
jointed, they can easily wriggle and twist through the
sand grains. Meiofaunal copepods feed by 'grazing' on
the microscopic gardens of diatoms and dinoflagellates that
grow on sand grains or other places. Some may also feed on
bacteria and fungi.

Rotifers and flatworms

There is another group of minute aquatic animals called ✺ rotifers. Although most rotifers live as freshwater plankton, some live as meiofauna in freshwater sediments and other places. The name rotifer means 'wheel bearer'. They get this name because of the hair-like structures, called cilia, which form a ring around their mouth. These cilia move in a way that looks like a spinning wheel.

✺ Flatworms have a long body that is flattened to look like a ribbon. Some flatworms are very large, but meiofaunal flatworms are less than 1 millimeter long. They live in a wide range of environments. Like many animals that live as meiofauna, flatworms have a very simple structure. Their small size allows them to survive without a heart, a skeleton, or gills.

Flatworms, such as this one, are common on rocky shores. Flatworms that live as meiofauna are very small. They are so thin that they do not need a heart or blood to transport food and oxygen around their bodies. Flatworms also have a very simple digestive system with only one opening.

cilia

Rotifers are most commonly
found in fresh water. Some rotifers
live between the grains of freshwater sediments.
Others live on damp patches of moss. They range in size from
40 micrometers to around 2 millimeters long. Rotifers have
rounded bodies that are usually transparent, but may show
the color of their last meal.

Some new 'wormy' things

Biologists studying meiofauna often find animals such as roundworms, copepods, rotifers and flatworms in their samples. These animals belong to phyla (groups) that biologists already know. However, the study of meiofauna has turned up animals biologists had never seen before. These new animals are so different from other animals that they are placed in their own phyla. Five of these animal phyla are only found as meiofauna. Discovering new groups of animals shows just how much we still have to learn about life on Earth.

As we found when looking at roundworms, a long body is ideal for life in the spaces between sand grains. Many of the newly discovered meiofauna also have long, worm-like bodies. Two examples of these are the ✷ Gnathostomulids and the ✷ Gastrotrichs. Like many other types of meiofauna, both gnathostomulids and gastrotrichs lack organs such as a heart, a skeleton, or gills. They are small enough to survive without these organs.

HOW DO YOU SAY IT?

gastrotrichs: **gas**-tro-trikes
gnathostomulids: nath-o-**stom**-u-lids

Members of the phylum (group) Gnathostomulida live in sandy sediments, on seaweeds and on seagrasses. They are sometimes called 'jaw worms' because of the spikes around their mouth. These spikes are used for feeding on diatoms, bacteria and fungi. Gnathostomulids have transparent bodies, from 300 micrometers to 1 millimeter long.

spikes
around
mouth

A second worm-like phylum found only as meiofauna is called the Gastrotricha. These animals have flat bodies with minute finger-like tubes that hold the animal in place. The smallest gastrotrichs are only 50 micrometers across. They live in many different aquatic environments, including sandy sediments and mossy pools. They feed on bacteria, diatoms and other small organisms and debris.

More small but bizarre creatures

The study of meiofauna has turned up some exciting and bizarre discoveries. In 1983, one such discovery was a new phylum called the ⚡ Loricifera. The word 'loricifera' means 'to have a corset or girdle'. These strange little animals are covered by a ring of six spiny plates (called lorica) that look a bit like a folded umbrella. So far, loricifers have been found in sand and gravel on the sea floor. They are so new to science that no one even knows what they eat.

Loricifers are between 200 and 400 micrometers long. They have a retractable head that is surrounded by long spines. As with many other types of meiofauna, loricifers do not have a heart or gills, but they do have a brain. Although loricifers may appear strange to human eyes, their shape and structure allow them to survive in the meiofaunal world.

Loricifers belong to a newly named animal phylum, the Loricifera. So far only 10 species have been discovered. They are so small that you would need a compound microscope to see one clearly. As shown in this compound-microscope image, loricifers have transparent bodies.

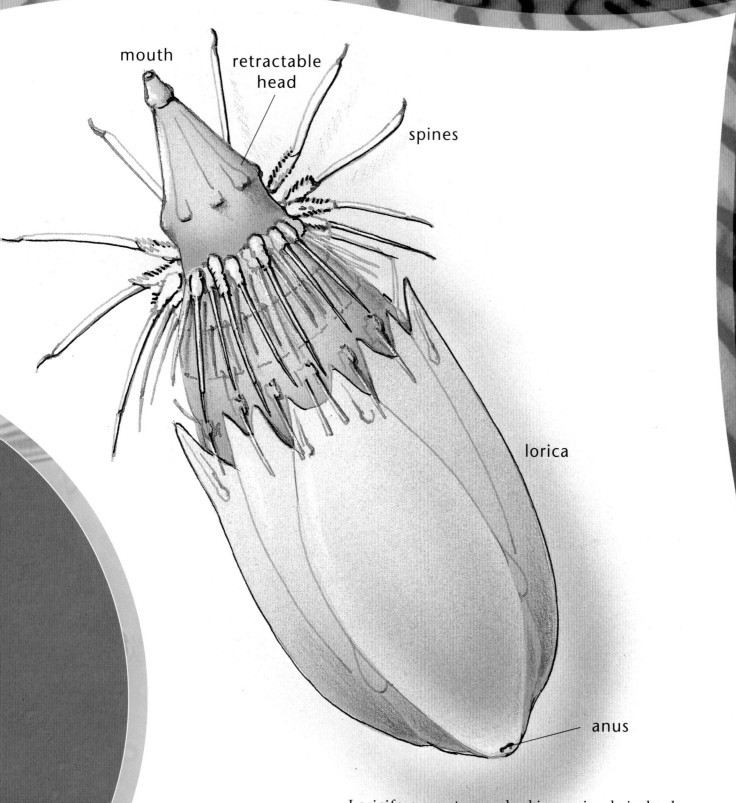

mouth

retractable
head

spines

lorica

anus

Loricifers are strange-looking animals indeed.
The retractable head has a tube-like mouth, but it
is not yet known what they eat. Now that these weird
little animals have been discovered, who knows what
other meiofauna are waiting to be revealed!

Water bears

eye

head

mouth

Another group of very small animals that only live as meiofauna are called ⚲ tardigrades. The word 'tardigrada' means 'slow stepper', and they get this name because of their unhurried movement. Because they have a rounded body and a bear-like way of moving, tardigrades are commonly known as ⚲ water bears. Around 800 species of water bears have been found. They live in the soil, and in freshwater and marine sediments. However, water bears are more commonly found on mosses and lichens.

HOW DO YOU SAY IT?

tardigrades: tar-**de**-grades

Water bears are not as strange to the human eye as loricifers. They have a distinctive head and four body segments. Each body segment has a pair of legs. The stumpy legs have claws that the water bear uses to grip things. Water bears also have the incredible ability to survive extreme conditions, such as being dried out or radiation—things that would kill humans and most other animals. After being dried out for 120 years, some water bears have come back to life when they were put in water!

Water bears range in size from 50 micrometers to around 1 millimeter in length. At this size we need a microscope to see them properly. This incredibly detailed picture was taken by a scanning electron microscope.

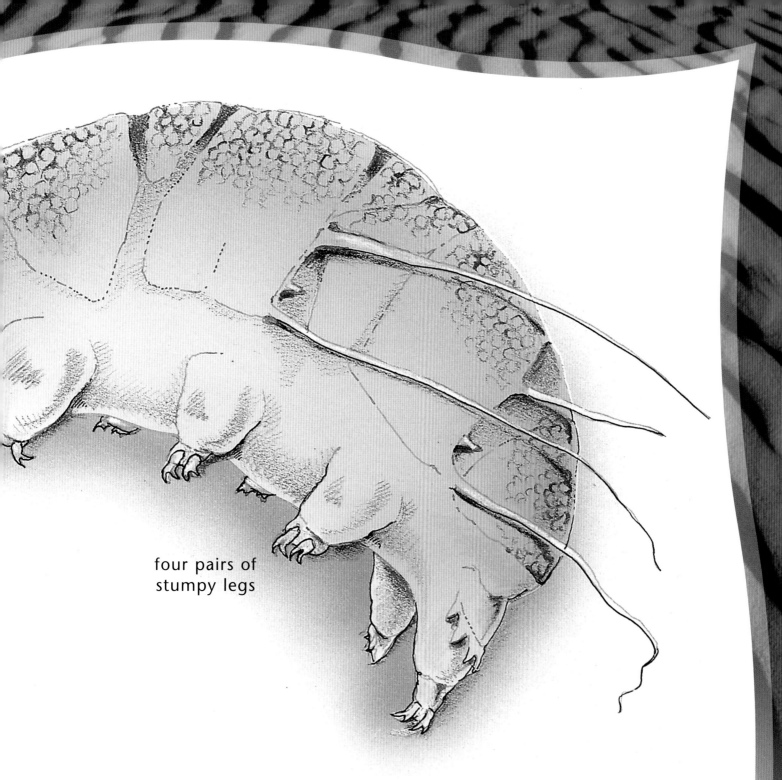

four pairs of
stumpy legs

Water bears have a rounded body and a distinctive head
that usually has two eyes and a mouth. The mouth is like
a tube because water bears eat liquid food. Many of the
water bears that live on mosses eat the liquid in the mosses.
Others feed on the body fluids of other meiofauna, such as
nematodes, rotifers or even other water bears.

Technology
Sieves and microscopes

Meiofauna live in both marine and freshwater environments. They can live between the grains that make up marine or freshwater sediments, and on other organisms, such as plants. In the sea, meiofauna can be found living on seagrasses and seaweeds. On land, they can be found on mosses and lichens. The methods used to collect meiofauna can be quite varied because they depend on where the meiofauna are found. Once collected, meiofauna needs to be separated from the material in which it lives. This is usually done with sieves.

Because meiofauna are so small you need a microscope to see them. A microscope makes small things look bigger. The first microscopes were developed 400 years ago in the Netherlands (Holland). Zacharias Jensen is believed to have built and used the first compound microscope (a microscope with two or more lenses). Another Dutch man, ✈ Anton van Leeuwenhoek, made a simple microscope with a single lens that was powerful enough to let him examine a range of microscopic organisms, including rotifers. Since then, microscopes have improved a lot and have helped scientists discover a great variety of microscopic life, including meiofauna.

HOW DO YOU SAY IT?

Leeuwenhoek: **lee**-an-**hook**

To separate meiofauna from sand, a sample is placed in a 1 millimeter sieve and washed with **distilled water**. The water, meiofauna and anything else that passes through the first sieve is then washed through a 42 micrometer sieve. While the water passes through, the meiofauna are too big to pass through the holes and are left behind in the sieve.

A compound microscope uses two or more lenses to magnify, or enlarge, the image of an object. A compound microscope requires light to be shone through an object. This means that the object must first be placed on a glass slide, a process that results in flat, two-dimensional images.

A second kind of microscope, called a scanning electron microscope (sem), uses a beam of electrons instead of light. These microscopes produce detailed three-dimensional images. Because electrons cannot show color, sem pictures are usually shown in black and white.

Profile of a marine scientist
Genefor Walker-Smith

As a child, Genefor Walker-Smith often spent her summer holidays at the beach, peering into rock pools and looking for interesting shells that had been washed ashore by the tide. For her 16th birthday, Genefor's parents gave her a wetsuit, mask, snorkel, fins and scuba diving lessons. These meant Genefor could explore the underwater world. There was so much to see, but the crabs and other crustaceans were always Genefor's favorites. By this time, Genefor had set her sights on becoming a marine biologist.

Science was always Genefor's favorite subject at school, so it is not surprising to find that she went on to study science at a university. She was then given the chance to work in the Crustacean Laboratory at Museum Victoria, where she spent her days studying crabs, crayfish and prawns. She soon discovered that there were hundreds, maybe even thousands, of different sorts of little crustaceans. Many of them had never been studied or named. Genefor chose to work on copepods—in particular, copepods that are members of the meiofaunal world and live on seagrass.

Seagrasses are marine plants that are usually found in shallow and sheltered bays. Meiofauna, such as copepods, that live on seagrass are the main source of food for young fish. If there were no copepods, the young fish would have nothing to eat and would not grow into adult fish.

Genefor Walker-Smith uses a microscope to look closely at the tiny copepods. Genefor makes very detailed drawings of each new copepod she discovers. She also writes a long description of each new type and gives it a special scientific name.

As well as drawing copepods and describing them, Genefor takes photographs, often with a scanning electron microscope. All of these things—the drawings, photographs, written descriptions and scientific names—are then used by other marine scientists to identify the copepods that they collect.

27

What meiofauna means to you

The value of biodiversity

The word biodiversity is relatively new. It means 'biological diversity'. In its simplest form, biodiversity means the number and variety of life forms found on Earth. Biologists have already counted around 1.5 million different species, but think there may be 30 million or more species on Earth not yet discovered. Most of the species that biologists already know about are larger organisms that belong to the animal, plant or fungi kingdoms. They do not know as much about the members of the Kingdom Protoctista and Kingdom Monera, and they know even less about the smaller members of the animal kingdom, such as meiofauna.

The fact that meiofauna are so small does not mean they are unimportant. Every living thing has its place—even the smallest things. Meiofauna are an important source of food for larger organisms. Meiofauna also help to keep our beaches clean. They do this by consuming rotting organic material that washes ashore. Because they are very sensitive to pollution, meiofauna are also thought to be valuable indicators of pollution and the health of an environment. Meiofauna, such as the newly discovered loricifers, are also of great interest. These weird little animals are only one example of the many hidden wonders of the meiofaunal world.

Sheltered muddy shores are often home to vast numbers of wading birds. Wading birds eat animals that survive by eating meiofauna. Without meiofauna the wading birds would not survive.

Meiofauna make up for being small by being present in incredible numbers. Billions of these minute animals may be present on the shore of a sandy beach. Despite being unseen by humans, meiofauna help to keep the beach clean.

Finding out more

Books like this one only give a brief introduction to a subject as broad as meiofauna. It is not easy to find other books about meiofauna, but some other general reference books are:

David Burnie, *Collins Eyewitness Science Life*, Harper Collins, 1994

Don Groves, *The Oceans: A Book of Questions and Answers*, John Wiley & Sons, 1989

Harry Breidahl, *Australia's Southern Shores*, Lothian Books, 1997

Lynn Margulis and Dorion Sagan, *What is Life?*, Weidenfeld and Nicolson, 1995

Lynn Margulis and Karlene V Schwawtz, *Five Kingdoms*, W H Freeman and Company, 1988

Miranda Macquitty, *Collins Eyewitness Guides Ocean*, Harper Collins, 1995

Paul A Haefner, *Exploring Marine Biology: Laboratory and Field Exercises*, D C Heath and Company, 1996

Information about meiofauna is hard to find on the web, but you may find the following sites useful to get you started:

www.ucmp.berkeley.edu/alllife/threedomains.html
A very comprehensive site about life on Earth. Have a look at the section on the animal kingdom.

whyfiles.news.wisc.edu/022critters/meiofauna.html
This site contains some interesting information about meiofauna.

As urls (web site addresses) may change, you may have trouble finding a site listed here. If this happens, you can still use the key words highlighted throughout the book to search for information about a topic.

Glossary

bacteria: Simple, single-celled microscopic organisms

compound microscope: A microscope with two or more lenses that makes an image of an object larger by passing light through it; this creates a color image

crustaceans: The name used by biologists to describe the group of animals that include crabs, crayfish and prawns

distilled water: Water that has been purified by being boiled and turned back into a liquid by condensation

lens: A piece of glass or other transparent substance that bends light rays. Often used to create a magnified image of an object

metric system: A system of measurement that uses the meter as its basic unit

organic: Any material made by a living thing

organisms: Living things

organs: Parts of an animal's body that perform special functions. The heart is an organ

parasites: Organisms that live on (or in) and feed upon an organism of another species

phytoplankton: Plant-like organisms that drift about in water, either in the sea or fresh water. Diatoms and dinoflagellates are examples of phytoplankton

plankton: Organisms that drift about in water, either in the sea or fresh water. Almost all are microscopic

scanning electron microscope: Also called a sem, this microscope uses a beam of electrons to make the image of an object larger. Sems produce a black and white image, but artificial colors can be added later if required

scuba: This stands for **s**elf **c**ontained **u**nderwater **b**reathing **a**pparatus. Scuba equipment allows a human to breathe underwater for a period of time

seagrasses: Flowering plants that live in the sea. Although not closely related to the grasses that live on land, seagrasses have proper roots, stems and leaves

sediments: Material that settles to the bottom of a liquid. Usually sand or mud

Index